CW00432077

How Hymns Shape Our Lives

Rosalind Brown

Vice Principal of the Ordained Local Ministry Scheme,
Diocese of Salisbury, and Academic Staff Member of the
Southern Theological Education and Training Scheme (STETS)

GROVE BOOKS LIMITED
RIDLEY HALL RD CAMBRIDGE CB3 9HU

Contents

The Cover Illustration is by Peter Ashton

Copyright © Rosalind Brown 2001

First Impression August 2001
ISSN 0262-799X
ISBN 1 85174 472 X

1
Introduction

Hymns and songs are not unique to Christian worship. However, as Christians we have our own heritage of hymns and songs that say something important about our own faith. In congregational worship they combine text and tune, the latter often having a powerful effect on the words. In personal prayer, texts are used with or without music. In exploring the role of hymns in our formation as Christians this book emphases the text rather than the tune, but we should not lose sight of the fact that normally the text is sung.

Although we assume that the rich variety of hymnody has always been available, it is only in the last one hundred and fifty years that we have had access to the hymnody of all previous generations, and to mass produced hymnbooks.[1] Initially, most hymns were doctrinal statements designed to reinforce the orthodox faith against heresy. In the Middle Ages poetry was used in the affective personal prayer of the period. After they split with the Church of England in the 1660s, the new Dissenting congregations introduced congregational song—it is said that Methodism was born in song. It was not until the nineteenth century that hymns were permitted in the Church of England, and only since the Second Vatican Council has congregational hymn singing been a major part of Roman Catholic worship. The genre of short choruses became popular through CSSM choruses for children, but has become more popular in recent years and been brought into church (rather than Sunday School) worship.[2] Recent changes in technology mean that new material can be disseminated quickly. An example of this is the almost instant popularity of *I the Lord of sea and sky* which is widely used across denominations.

Whether we realize it or not, hymns affect us.[3] They can—to paraphrase a well known saying—reach places in us that other words cannot reach and can go on working long after the service is ended. Something as simple as a song sticking in our mind all day, or the cumulative effect of singing, may change our way of thinking or living. We are being formed. But how do hymns shape our lives? How can we use them to deepen our life with God? How can those who choose what is sung in church do so wisely, aware of what the effect might be?

---

1   The Latin and Greek hymns of the early church were lost to use until they were translated in the nineteenth century, when many German Reformation hymns were also translated. The invention of the printing press had helped to distribute words more widely, but many people were illiterate. Although folk singing embedded words in people's memories, in church metrical psalms were lined out with a cantor singing a line and the people singing it back. This tedious process slowed the singing and split phrases so that memorisation was difficult.

2   On worship songs, see Victoria Cooke, *Understanding Songs in Renewal* (Grove Renewal booklet R 4).

3   For the purpose of this booklet, songs and choruses are included within the phrase 'hymns' unless otherwise indicated.

2
Teaching And Formation

Hymns have different purposes. Hymns enable congregational participation in worship; they teach scriptural and theological truths, provoke memories of God's past acts and give people the vocabulary of faith. They tell the Christian story, especially to children, evoke a response of devotion or initial commitment, and inculcate Christian virtues. They keep hope alive in the face of persecution and oppression, and stir action against social ills. They evoke emotions, comfort us or strengthen our resolve; they give us usable words to borrow and make our own, words that can be used in many different situations including words with which to pray in times of distress. It is to the role of hymns in teaching that we turn first.

Doctrine, Theology and Bible

The earliest hymns shaped the lives of their singers by teaching orthodox doctrine, so empowering them to oppose heresy (which was also being sung). We hear of rival choirs of Christians and Arians[4] taking theological pot shots at each other over the city walls, drowning each other out, sometimes coming to blows in what amounted to a musical war. Augustine wrote, 'It was then (during the Arian heresy when there was alarm in the city) that the practice of singing hymns and psalms was introduced, in keeping with the usage of the Eastern churches, to revive the flagging spirits of the people during their long and cheerless watch. Ever since then the custom has been retained…'[5]

Alongside baiting the enemy and maintaining their own spirits, early Christians sang the truth into their lives. Thanks to the nineteenth century translators, many of these early hymns have been recovered. They can shape our beliefs too as they help us to absorb basic doctrine, as in the fifth century hymn which disposes of Arianism in the first five words:

Of the Father's love begotten / ere the world became to be
He is Alpha and Omega / he the source, the ending he…

It is not only the early hymns that immerse us in doctrinal truth, Charles Wesley's *Hark the herald angels sing* has embedded the theology of the Incarnation into people's vocabulary:

---

4   Arianism was an early heresy which denied the divinity of Christ, saying that he was created in time by God, rather than begotten from eternity.
5   Augustine, *Confessions* IX.7.

Christ by highest heaven adored / Christ the everlasting Lord,
Late in time behold him come, / offspring of a Virgin's womb.
Veiled in flesh the Godhead see![6] / Hail, the incarnate Deity!
Pleased as Man with man to dwell, / Jesus our Emmanuel.

The problem for our TV generation is the density of the language of these doctrinal hymns. However, when linked with a familiar tune, the words can work their way into our memories, making us theologically literate. For instance, Samuel Crossman's text, *My song is love unknown*, with its lines 'love to the loveless shown that they might lovely be,' introduces Abelard's understanding of God's love drawing love out of us.[7] By contrast, Mrs Alexander's explanation of the death of Christ in *There is a green hill far away* is based on Anselm.[8] As this hymn is one on which British children have been raised in the past (although it is barely known in most American churches), most British churches probably have congregations whose understanding of the atonement is informed by the unpayable debts of honour of medieval feudal society. Timothy Rees' hymn, *O crucified Redeemer*, expounds the twentieth century understanding that Christ's passion continues today in our world, and challenges us to live with our eyes open to Christ's presence in suffering:

The groaning of creation, / wrung out by pain and care,
The anguish of a million hearts / that break in dumb despair;
O crucified Redeemer, / these are your cries of pain;
O may they break our selfish hearts / and love come in to reign.

Hymns introduce biblical as well as theological vocabulary, in phrases like 'When I tread the verge of Jordan,' 'Here I raise my Ebeneezer,' 'Jerusalem the golden with milk and honey blest,' 'Within the veil,' 'Zion, city of our God,' 'O Sabbath rest by Galilee' and 'Christ is our cornerstone.' There can be problems when biblical vocabulary is assumed or taken out of context—many people must have wondered what an Ebeneezer is that they are raising, and understanding the line in a recent chorus 'I will dance, I will sing…and I'll become even more undignified than this' depends upon familiarity with the exchange between David and Michal in 2 Samuel 6.21–22.

---

6   There has been some debate about this phrase which, taken on its own, appears to deviate from orthodox doctrine (was Christ's divinity *veiled* by his flesh?). However, taken in its poetic context, it is generally thought to be acceptable.

7   Peter Abelard (1079–1142) drew on medieval ideas of courtly love to describe how Christ's death on the cross for us is such an example of his love that we should respond with our own love. He described Christ as 'my lemmon (lover) swete.'

8   Anselm (1033–1109), Archbishop of Canterbury, interpreted the atonement in the terms of feudal society's honour system in which human sin has dishonoured God and requires the restoration of God's honour either by repayment in full and more, or punishment. Only Jesus had the resources (in his divinity) and the obligation (in his humanity) to pay it and so restore the intended relationship between God and humans that sin had severed.

Other hymns paraphrase, and thus teach, the biblical text. *While shepherds watched* is one of the earliest such surviving paraphrases, along with the metrical paraphrase of Psalm 100, *All people that on earth do dwell*. *While shepherds watched* adds nothing to the biblical account. We sing it as narrative and do not give voice to our own response to the news of the birth of a saviour. Later narratives bowed to artistic licence and added a congregational response. Thus the shepherds in *The first nowell* see a star and are outside on a cold winter's night, the last verse expresses response to what has gone before. Other examples of paraphrased biblical texts include versions of Psalm 23; *The king of love my shepherd is* introduces into this Old Testament text a reference to 'thy cross before to guide me'. *How lovely on the mountains* puts Isaiah 52 into our memories, while versions of *How lovely is thy dwelling place* derive from Psalm 84. Many choruses are simply verses of Scripture set to music—for example *Seek ye first*, *Worthy is the Lamb* and *Holy, holy, holy is the Lord*. Artistic licence continues. A recent chorus addresses Jesus as the 'apple of my eye,'[9] despite the fact that in Scripture it is we who are the apple of God's eye.[10]

Due to the proliferation of translations of the Bible, there is no longer a common biblical vocabulary. Despite this, hymns still put biblical language and images on our lips and embed them in our memory. In doing so they may—thanks largely to the tune—also insert punctuation or interpretation that helps or hinders the understanding. Try reading Isaiah 40 (particularly in the AV) without Handel's Messiah punctuating and interpreting the text for you.

John Wesley knew the power of hymns to teach the faith and evoke commitment. In the preface to the *1780 Handbook* he wrote:

> [The hymnbook] is large enough to contain all the important truths of our most holy religions, whether speculative or practical; yea, to illustrate them all, and to prove them both by Scripture and reason...The hymns are not carelessly jumbled together but carefully ranged under proper heads, according to the experience of real Christians. So that this book is in effect a little body of experimental and practical divinity...I would recommend (it) to every truly pious reader: as a means of raising or quickening the spirit of devotion, of confirming his faith, of enlivening his hope, and of kindling or increasing his love to God and man.[11]

Personal Devotion, Commitment and Formation

Hymns have a long tradition not only as congregational song but in personal devotion. The British tradition of printing the words as poetry, separately from the music, helps. Americans find it harder to use hymns as personal prayer

---

9   *As the deer pants for the water.*
10 Deut 32.10; Ps 17.8; Zech 2.8.
11 Preface to the 1780 handbook, Paragraphs 4 and 8.

because in their hymnals words are printed under the music, thus separating syllables and destroying the line structure of the verse. Even if we do not use a hymn book in prayer, we may draw on the words of hymns at times to give us usable words when our own will not come, assuring us that we are not alone in facing these hopes or fears.

Medieval spiritual directors urged people to read accounts of the life of Christ that were punctuated by exhortations and questions to help those praying to imagine themselves in the biblical scene. This prayer was aided by the new ability of artists to paint life-like representations of Christ. Texts like *Stabat Mater* and *O sacred head, sore wounded* focused prayer on the scenes portrayed. Today we can use texts like *Ah holy Jesus, how hast thou offended?* to enter the story in a similar way, since the questions are provided for us in the text. The radical Reformation switch from visual to word-based piety removed the images used but did not deter this way of contemplative prayer. Instead of relying on visual art, *When I survey the wondrous cross* paints a word picture, inviting us to 'survey' in unhurried devotion and to

See from his head, his hands, his feet,/sorrow and love flow mingled down

and then to ask ourselves:

Did e'er such love and sorrow meet/or thorns compose so rich a crown?

The final verse of *My song is love unknown* expresses the same sentiment,

Here might I stay and sing/no story so divine,
Never was love, dear king,/never was grief like thine,
This is my friend in whose sweet praise/I all my days could gladly spend.

Hymns like these, when used as personal prayer, express our desire for a deeper and richer devotional life. They have formative potential as they lead us to varied responses—to imitate Christ, to share his suffering, to give ourselves to him, and to amend our life.

Lines from many hymns can be helpful in the practice of *lectio divina*. This way of meditating on biblical and other texts aims to read not in quantity but in depth. The reader stops when a text strikes the heart and uses that as the focus of extended reflection and rumination. This method can be introduced to a congregation using hymns like *My song is love unknown, Praise to the holiest in the height* or *Love divine, all loves excelling.*

Hymns that began as personal prayers and can be reclaimed as such include Bernard of Clairvaux's *Jesus, the very thought of thee* and George Herbert's *Teach me, my God and king* and *Let all the world in every corner sing.* Bishop Thomas Ken wrote *Awake, my soul, and with the sun thy daily course of duty run* and *Glory to thee, my God, this night* as personal morning and evening prayers that provided him with a structure for an inventory of life. This devotion needs slow attentive reflection which is not possible when personal exhortations fly past in the singing of a hymn. When praying slowly we can, with Ken:

> Redeem thy mis-spent time that's past/and live this day as if thy last;
> Improve thy talent with due care/for the great day thyself prepare.
> Let all thy converse be sincere/thy conscience as the noon-day clear;
> Think how all-seeing God thy ways/and all thy secret thoughts surveys.

And in the evening as we review the day, we can pray:

> Forgive me, Lord, for thy dear Son/the ill that I this day have done,
> That with the world, myself, and thee/I, ere I sleep, at peace may be.

Later, Ken and Herbert's very specific rooting of holiness in daily actions gave way to holiness couched in the general language of consecration to and love of Jesus, walking with and staying close to him. These texts point to holiness that is principally concerned with the dynamics of the heart rather than specific actions. A refrain like 'Trust and obey, for there's no other way / to be happy in Jesus, but to trust and obey' reinforces this understanding of holiness as a heart attitude, in contrast to the seventeenth century divines' emphasis on the practical implications of a holy life. *More holiness give me* prays for holiness and other attributes like patience, faith, joy and zeal; although the hymn implies these virtues are received as gift, in practice we grow in them through facing situations where we need them. Hymns like these may assume holiness is a gift received and an attitude of the heart, but when the prayer is answered we will find there are profound implications for the way we live our lives.

The Formation of a Worshipping People

In the nineteenth century, Friederich Schleiermacher wrote:

> There is so much discussion as to how one can again revive the common expression of the religious life; but it scarcely occurs to anyone that the best results could most easily be achieved if one would again place song in a more correct relation to the word. What the word has clarified, the tone must vivify, must transport straightway as a harmony into the innermost recesses of one's being, and there must hold it fast.[12]

Hymns bed the word into a congregation, and at the same time unite it—when we sing together we are drawn together and formed into one body. We know

---

12   Friederich Schleiermacher, *Die Weinachtsfeier* quoted in P H Pfatteicher, *Liturgical Spirituality* (Valley Forge PA: Trinity Press International, 1997).

the effects of *Cwm Rhonnda* at sports fixtures or *Jerusalem* at the Last Night of the Proms. Words and music also have power to whip up emotion inappropriately, something Hitler knew well. National hymns, in particular, are open to this danger; Old Testament prophets must turn in their graves to hear us pledge 'the love that asks no questions' to our country. Positively, the Wesleys, the American revivalists and Billy Graham used music in their evangelistic missions and revivals to draw the gathering together and to prepare people for the message.

Singing hymns of the faith together, individuals are formed into a worshipping and praising people. George Herbert's phrase, 'The church with psalms must shout' expresses the Psalm-based worship of the Church of England in the seventeenth century. As already noted, once the Dissenting churches broke away after the Act of Uniformity in 1662 hymnody changed. Isaac Watts kept hold of the biblical text but wrote words that enabled people to express their devotion. He had complained to his father that 'to see the dull Indifference, the negligent and the thoughtless Air that sits upon the Faces of the whole Assembly while the Psalm is on their lips, might tempt even a charitable Observer to suspect the fervency of inward Religion.'[13] His father challenged him to do better. Watts' resulting blend of biblical tradition and personal devotion crossed the Rubicon from objective paraphrase towards subjective engagement with the text, as in *When I survey the wondrous cross*.

Other writers followed Watts, resulting in texts like *Hark the glad sound! The Saviour comes* (Dodderidge), *Love divine* and *And can it be?* (Wesley). People singing these hymns used biblical language either by allusion or direct quotation, but also made their own response. We can see this in Cowper's hymn, *Hark, my soul, it is the Lord* which uses Scriptures in a quantity that would have warmed the hearts of people a century earlier, yet has moved light years away from their rigid paraphrasing into a new realm that combines several biblical texts, interacts with them and applies them to the individual who makes a personal response:

> Hark my soul! It is the Lord!/'Tis the Saviour, hear his word.
> Jesus speaks, and speaks to thee,/'Say, poor sinner, lov'st thou me?
> I delivered thee when bound/and, when wounded, healed thy wound;
> Sought thee wandering, set thee right/turned thy darkness into light.
> Can a woman's tender care/cease towards the child she bare?
> Yes, she may forgetful be,/yet will I remember thee.'
> Lord, it is my chief complaint/that my love is weak and faint;
> Yet I love thee, and adore,/O for grace to love thee more!

Because hymnody expresses response to God, there will always be the human voice in the hymn. Some 'I' texts form us as a worshipping congregation as together we tell what has happened to us as members of the community and

---

13   Isaac Watts, *Works* iv.253.

encourage one another with our experiences of God's goodness and grace. Examples include *I cannot tell, Great is thy faithfulness* and *I will sing the wondrous story*. Other 'I' texts depend not on shared action or experience but on personal feeling or desire. They focus not on what God has done or said, or even what happens to me as a result, but on what I *feel* in myself, what I *want* to do. These texts have made a transition from hymns that root us in the biblical story, out of which we respond to God, towards hymns which may assume but do not articulate that biblical foundation, focusing instead on the singer's personal need and response. Some of this is terrible, indulgent verse that mercifully does not survive more than one edition of a hymnal. An early example by Augustus Toplady, author of *Rock of ages*, includes the words, 'O precious side-hole's cavity / I want to spend my life in thee.' Some much-loved Victorian hymns come perilously close to escapist sentimentality. The refrain of *I come to the garden alone* says 'and he walks with me, and he talks with me, / and he tells me I am his own, / and the joy we share as we tarry there / none other has ever known.' *Beneath the cross of Jesus* seeks shelter under the cross, 'content to let the world go by…' Although these desires may be very real, they cannot be the basis of corporate worship.

Two recent songs with similar first lines illustrate this point: *Jesus put this song into our hearts* gives a very basic explanation for why we sing whereas, *I've got a love song in my heart* simply expresses the singer's emotions. Some worship songs move a stage further by no longer telling others of our feelings or experience but singing about them directly to God, oblivious to the presence or absence of other people. *I need you more, more than yesterday, I have come to love you, I'm so secure,* may be true for me on the basis of what I feel but, without an explanation of what God has done to evoke this feeling, it cannot automatically connect us with others. Hymns that speak of what we feel without explaining *why* that is so belong in private devotion. Their inclusion in corporate worship can only be formative by forming an 'in group' and outsiders who do not share the feelings. What a contrast with hymns that expand our vision of the church's worship, on earth and in heaven, in texts like *All people that on earth do dwell* and *Crown him with many crowns*.

Even in personal prayer, these self-focused hymns lack formative power since their roots are not in the Christian story. Although it may produce great fervency initially, much like the wheat sown among rocks (Mark 4.16–17), devotion based on feeling alone will not stand the test of time and thus is not formative in any permanent way. True Christian formation is expressed in devotion that continues when feelings go, and many hymns provide for this. Thus, in *When I survey*, Isaac Watts also talks about love and maintains the intensity of his devotion in the first person singular whilst enabling others to join the hymn by explaining the foundation of that love. Together we can sing about the love as we describe it to one another:

See from his head, his hands, his feet,/sorrow and love flow mingled down.
Did e'er such love and sorrow meet,/or thorns compose so rich a crown?...
Love so amazing, so divine,/demands my soul, my life, my all.

In this text, and others like it—for example *And can it be*—feelings are strong,
but they are not the point of contact between singers of the hymn. Instead the
actions and love of Christ are what singers hold in common. Participation in the
hymn does not depend upon a person *feeling* God's love or their reciprocal love
for God, but upon shared affirmation of the facts of who God is and what God
has done.

Watts knew the inadequacy of the solitary voice to express praise to God
when he yearned, 'O for a thousand tongues to sing my dear Redeemer's praise.'
In the church's formation lies our own formation as individuals. It is much more
helpful to have such hymns of the church as a resource than to be dependent on
songs that just say what I feel in my better moments. As the church sings together, she is formed in the truth of the words:

> Christ is made the sure foundation,/Christ the head and corner stone
> Chosen of the Lord and precious,/binding all the church in one;
> Holy Zion's help for ever,/and her confidence alone.

As we are formed together, we are also formed individually. In the fourth century Athanasius wrote:

> One who sings praise beautifully brings rhythm to the soul. By this means
> one leads the soul from disproportion to proportion. The result is that the
> encouraged soul loses fear, thinks on good things, and embraces the future.
> Gaining composure by the singing of praises, the soul transcends the life of
> passions, and joyfully beholds according to the mind of Christ the most ex-
> cellent thoughts.[14]

The television programme *Songs of Praise* keeps a selection of hymns in the pub-
lic repertoire. It provides an opportunity for people on their own to sing along
and feel part of a much larger congregation. This can be helpful for people who
are house-bound, for whom watching *Songs of Praise* functions as a substitute
for attending church—and it seems to be hymns, not the liturgy or the sermon,
that form us and remind us that we members of a worshipping people.

---

14   Quoted in G Huck (ed), *A Sourcebook About Liturgy* (Chicago: Liturgy Training Publications, 1994) p 54.

3
Identity, Memory, Hope and Action

Hymns can carry the faith even for the unchurched. When planning weddings or funerals, people who do not attend church are likely to choose hymns they learned as children. Hymns are significant markers of events and experiences. Later in life, these may serve as reminders of the original event—be it an episode in childhood, a wedding, or even a particular person. Anyone helping with hospital services will discover that patients with sports injuries on the men's surgical wards often choose *Abide with me* because of its associations. A hymn that carries meaning can shape lives at further transition moments, if handled sensitively by a minister who is alert to the power of hymns to evoke memories. Whether these hymns express nostalgia or devotion, there is always the possibility of rekindling the flame that led to the hymn being significant in the first place. In that respect these hymns function both as containers of experience and as places of encounter.

Because a life-time of singing embeds words in our subconscious, we need to pay attention to what people today are storing for future use. Just as many elderly people will mouth the words of Psalm 23 or the Lord's Prayer when a minister says it with them, so hymns like *The Lord's my shepherd*, *Rock of ages*, or *The old rugged cross* are often quoted, particularly by the older generation. Most older people have heard that eggs can be boiled to perfection while *Nearer, my God, to thee* is sung! In times of trouble, when words will not come spontaneously, hymns often give words with which to pray. Apart from bringing comfort, they provide a way of bringing our distress into contact with the language of faith. This helps to explain the enormous popularity of hymns like *Just as I am* and *Lead kindly light amid the encircling gloom*. A hymn written in 1915 provided a wartime evening prayer:

> Be with all the dear ones/whom we miss tonight,
> In the hours of danger/keep them calm and bright.
> From the camp and trenches,/from the battle plain,
> From the mine-sown ocean/bring them safe again.

The time when, perhaps more than any other, we need words to help us pray is when we are face to face with death. Benedict said that we should keep our death always before us, and hymns can help us to do that. The classic hymn in this respect is *Abide with me, fast falls the eventide*. Victorian hymnals had extensive sections on death and dying, including hymns for children in an age when most had siblings who died in infancy. Even hymns of praise did not duck the ever-present fact of death, *Praise, my soul, the king of heaven* has a rarely sung verse:

Frail as summer's flowers we flourish/blows the wind and it is gone.
But while mortals rise and perish/God endures unchanging on.

The First World War contributed new hymns that focused on death as sacrifice for others, thus assuring the bereaved that the death was not in vain. Dying people have to turn to this mixed bag of older hymns, for few contemporary texts help us prepare for death or face death as a fact of life. The few recent songs that allude to death tend either to trample it triumphantly underfoot or express preparedness to die for the sake of the gospel—hardly a major possibility in our culture at the moment. Pastorally, we can only wonder what problems this is building in for the future. The next generation will have to prepare to die unfamiliar with hymns that give us vocabulary with which to speak of death with faith.

Memory and the Story of Faith

There is a genre of hymnody that shapes Christian lives by employing the biblical narrative to turn our world inside out. These are the spirituals that were born out of slavery. Spirituals reconfigured the world so that slavery was seen in the light of the norm of the biblical story of God's deliverance. People with no human freedom sang of their identity as children of God. Just as the Old Testament prophets mocked the idols of their day ('Bel bows down, Nebo stoops'[15]), so the spirituals mocked the slave holders and kept the slaves' faith alive. 'As they sang, the future become now, and the motivation to persist was strengthened. Beneath the surface of jubilant celebration, the agenda for the life of the future as well as the life of the present remained consistently present.'[16]

Such hymns not only looked forward to hope, they looked backward to memory and kept that alive. Singing the songs of Zion kept alive the memory of Jerusalem as the author of Psalm 137 laments so vividly when these songs were abused and mocked. Slaves and exiles know that if they are to keep a sense of their identity they have to keep singing their song. To forget one's song is to forget one's story: 'Now I can look at you, Mr Loomis, and see a man who done forgot his song. Forgot how to sing it. A fellow forget that and he forget who he is. Forget how he's supposed to mark down life.'[17]

Memory has immense formative power. The book of Deuteronomy insists that the people tell the story, passing it on to their children in order to form and build fidelity in them, 'so as neither to forget the things that your eyes have seen nor to let them slip from your mind all the days of your life' (Deut 4.9). Moses used song to do this (Exodus 15, Deut 31.19). *Now thank we all our God* is a poignant example of a memory-provoking hymn that takes us back beyond our present circumstances in order to be formed by God's longer and greater story. It was

---

15   Isaiah 46.1.
16   Arthur C Jones, *Wade in the Water: the Wisdom of the Spirituals* (Maryknoll NY: Orbis, 1993) p 104.
17   *ibid*, p 37.

written in the seventeenth century during the appalling suffering of the Thirty Years War by a pastor who spent most of his ordained life burying thousands of victims of the war and resulting famines. In those horrific times, people confronted the terror by singing of God,

> Who wondrous things has done,/in whom his world rejoices,
> Who from our mother's arms/has blessed us on our way
> With countless gifts of love/and still is ours today.
> O may this bounteous God/through all our life be near us...

The words helped to restore faith and renew vision by keeping alive the bigger story that could so easily be lost in the daily anguish the people endured.

All of us can be formed by hymns in this way. As we sing the story of God's character and acts, we pass on the story. During the Easter Vigil the Exsultet scoops us up across the centuries and incorporates us in the action since, 'this is the night when all who believe in Christ are delivered from the gloom of sin,' just as Jews, year after year, are reminded that 'this is the night when the Lord brought our ancestors out of Egypt.' Hymns like *Tell out my soul the greatness of the Lord* and *Didn't my Lord deliver Daniel* bring God's acts in the past into our experience and forbid us to remain as passive observers. Instead they write us into that history and insist that we live and act in the light of it.

The Prophetic Edge of Hymnody

In contrast with this evoking of memory and direct appropriation of the biblical story, other hymns shape lives by holding up models of behaviour to emulate. Within the context of worship, they carry a tacit endorsement that this is indeed a godly way to live. The themes range widely. *Take time to be holy, speak oft with thy Lord* identifies holiness with withdrawal from the world to perform certain devotional acts. *Do something new, Lord* lays all at God's feet and asks to be shown how to act. And *When cross the crowded ways of life* seeks God amidst the squalor and suffering of the urban poor. At their best these hymns model an holistic spirituality; at their worst they baptize contemporary cultural values rather than modelling the Christian virtues. Children's hymns are particularly prone to this latter pitfall, especially in their insistence that children emulate the idealized image of Jesus the child who does not cry (*Away in a manger*) and always obeys his mother (*Once in royal David's city*)!

Some hymns aim to provoke us to action on specific social ills. The earliest date from the anti-slavery campaigns, but by the end of the nineteenth century hymnwriters had turned to another social ill, drink. No hymnal was complete without its temperance hymns which pulled no punches in describing the behaviour required. More than one began, 'Keep thyself pure.' Sung in a crowded room at a temperance meeting, these hymns had enormous emotional and formative power. Mission hymns, particularly in the Victorian period, inspired many people to pray and to give to overseas missions, perhaps to offer themselves for missionary service. A TV programme on the protest movement included an interview with three social activist siblings upon whom 'liberal politics, pacifism, and Methodist hymns have left an indelible mark.'[18] The siblings described how the cumulative effect of singing Methodist missionary hymns, reinforced by their parents' example of social awareness and action, created a feeling of being a small band of pilgrims marching onwards to a better world. One said of these hymns, 'It does root into you.'

At the turn of the twentieth century hymns spoke of human suffering and prayed for God's kingdom to come, but rarely ventured too far in challenging singers to act themselves. In the 1920s, Geoffrey Studdert-Kennedy wrote of Christ's coming in the midst of factories and mines, while more recently *A cry in the night* referred to homelessness at a time when 'Cathy Come Home' had hit the nation. *We have a dream, we have a dream* was written just after Martin Luther King's speech, and Fred Kaan's *Sing we a song of high revolt*, refers to the Magnificat being sung in Council flats. These contemporary heirs of the anti-slavery and temperance hymns challenge us to make and act on links between the current social issues and our faith, putting them into a theological frame of reference.

Not all contemporary hymns challenge us in this way. *God of concrete, God of steel* is one of the most quoted, rarely sung hymns of the 1960s. It states what God is God or Lord of—concrete, steel, piston, wheel, motorway, mail, physics and research—in factual terms but it does not wrestle with the connection between them and God, except to say that they are God's. Had the hymn gone on to explore, for example, the incredible implications of God being a God of the atom or of girders, then the images could be used creatively and formatively. There are many potentially formative images that are not developed; these include God as road-builder, creating a way for us to walk on in our pilgrimage, or the power of the God of girders to bear loads, bridge gaps and to hold together opposites in society. Not all metaphors and images in hymns need to be spelled out—some are more powerful if understated—but some need to be elaborated if they are to work in the brief space of time allowed to a line of a hymn.

Recently the Wild Goose Songs from Iona have taken known folk tunes that already belong to the people, and used them to continue the prophetic challenge. For example, *Inspired by love and anger* is set to *Salley Gardens*. These tunes take hymns out of church and into the common vocabulary, something Reformation hymnwriters did too, including the person who borrowed a German drinking song (now known as the Passion Chorale) for *O sacred head, sore wounded*. In the introduction to one Iona song book the editors write, 'We hope this material will help preserve Christians…from the seductiveness of easy praise which maximizes the feel-good factor at the expense of biblical faith. And we pray that

---

18 'The Rise and Sprawl of the Middle Classes' BBC 2, March 2001.

it will help ensure that the curtain between the sacred and the secular, which Jesus ripped apart at the cross, will never be the object of religious mending.'[19]

Hymns have always had a prophetic function. Nearly three thousand years ago God's lament over the people (Isaiah 5) was couched in song. The formational power of these prophetic hymns lies in the challenge to bring the gospel and the culture together, their insistence that what we believe cannot be divorced from the way we live. They introduce a social aspect to holiness and commitment that is absent from earlier hymns. If pre-nineteenth century hymns referred to aspects of human liberation, it was usually in terms of God's action ('he sets the prisoner free') not human responsibility to act. In contrast, prophetic hymns insist upon the demands of the gospel, and like the sixties protest songs to which some late twentieth century Christian songs are cousins, they can have great formative power in motivating young (and old) people to take action.

Hymns and the Formation of Children and Young People

Children's behaviour has been the target of many hymns from the eighteenth century onwards. Authors slipped many a moral lesson in, sometimes blatantly. And so we have such 'improving verses' as:

Do no sinful action / speak no angry word,
Ye belong to Jesus / children of the Lord.

Christ is kind and gentle / Christ is pure and true,
And his little children / must be holy too.

Little children must be quiet / when to the holy church they go,
They must sit with serious faces, / must not play or whisper low.

For the church is God's own Temple / where men go for praise and prayer,
And the great God will not love them / who forget His presence there.

This use of religious language in hymns to enforce good behaviour raises the question of how we understand the formational process of hymns in children's lives. It is fascinating to compare the prefaces to two collections for children, dating from 1790 and 1986. In 1790 John Wesley wrote in the preface to an edition of Charles Wesley's children's hymns, 'There are two ways of writing or speaking to children; the one is to let ourselves down to them; the other, to lift them up to us. Dr Watts wrote in the former way, and has succeeded admirably well, speaking to children as children, and leaving them as he found them. The following hymns are written on the other plan: they contain strong and manly sense, yet expressed in such plain and easy language as even children can un-

---

19 J L Bell and G Maule, *Love and Anger* (Glasgow: Wild Goose Publications, 1997) Introduction.

derstand. But when they do understand them, they will be children no longer, only in years and stature.'

In 1986 the preface to *Junior Praise* stated, 'Singing should be fun…we would strongly encourage musical involvement by children as well as singing the words…Our overriding principle in offering this book for use in day schools and Sunday Schools is that children should be encouraged through music to understand that God wants them to enjoy the experience of knowing, loving, serving and worshipping him. The discipline which such Christian commitment makes possible will enable children to grow up as men and women of integrity in a world full of increasingly difficult moral dilemmas and temptations.'[20]

The hymns in the eighteenth-century book address children as much as God, aiming to produce Christian maturity in even a young child. In contrast, the twentieth century book aims to create a level of comfort in God's presence that will mature into discipleship and bear fruit in informed Christian living. Both know the formative power of hymns for children, but harness it differently.

The twentieth century was not immune from the use of hymnody to reinforce norms of behaviour in children. In 1925, *Songs of Praise* provided more hymns intended to shape the conduct of their singers and to build a nation that would help to bring in the kingdom of God on earth. This hymnal was used widely in schools—a survey in the 1960s revealed that 62% of the schools used it.[21] Generations of school children sang texts that advocate certain types of behaviour. Secular poems with morally uplifting sentiments were commandeered as Christian hymns and shorn of their original contexts: *Turn back, O man, foreswear thy foolish ways, Build up heroic lives, Once to every man and nation comes the moment to decide* (part of an 1844 poem about the Mexican civil war) and the anti-slavery hymn *O brother man fold to thy heart thy brother*.

By the early 1960s, the most frequently sung hymns in schools were *All people that on earth do dwell; Let us with a gladsome mind; He who would valiant be; Praise, my soul, the king of heaven; The king of love my shepherd is*; and *We plough the fields and scatter*.[22] All this has changed, it seems. The hymns and songs that most children sing today are very different. Returns by schools involved in the Christian Copyright Licence scheme show that, between April and September 1999, the most used songs were *One more step along the world I go, Light up the fire, Who put colours in the rainbow?* and *Lord of the Dance*.[23] This licence only applies to a particular sector of the total body of hymnody, but nevertheless shows that, if what children sing today is formative for the rest of their lives, clearly their faith will rest on foundations different from those of earlier generations.

---

20 *Junior Praise* (Basingstoke: Marshall, Morgan and Scott, 1986).
21 Slater, J T, *Bulletin of the University of Leeds Institute of Education,* November 1961.
22 *ibid.*
23 Information from Christian Copyright Licensing Scheme, 2000.

4

What Are We Singing Today?

A recent survey of what was sung in British churches in the last half of 2000[24] suggests that we sing an enormous range of hymns and songs that express a wide spectrum of theological and devotional perspectives. There were 1345 different hymns and songs sung among the 6517 'singings' reported in the survey, and the most popular hymn was only sung 1% of the time.[25] This immense range suggests that we lack a common corpus of hymnody. The resulting formational effects are likely to be both broader and more local, since there is more scope for one church to sing very different hymns from its neighbour. What inspires a church's diet of hymns can be anything from the minister's personal preference to what the musicians can play. While some ministers pay careful attention to the formative power of the words they choose, others ignore it entirely, so that the Christian formation of a congregation through hymnody becomes, by default, a hit and miss affair.

The survey showed that many churches have two hymn books, one traditional and one contemporary. As hymn books have different selections of hymns and thus shape their singers' lives differently, two congregations in one church can be shaped quite differently by their hymns, even to the extent of having entirely different vocabularies of hymnody. The contents page or subject index of a hymnal can reveal much about its emphases and thus its potential formative effect on those using it. Some have many subsections of hymns that refer to personal devotion to Christ, others have many subsections of hymns concerned with Christian living in the world; some have many mission hymns, others have many that praise God.

Another perspective on the formational effect of hymn books can be gained by looking at the most common ways of speaking of God. Taking the first word of hymns, there is remarkable consistency between books: 1–2% of hymns begin by addressing God as 'Father'; 3–5% begin by addressing Jesus Christ, and less than 1% begin by addressing the Holy Spirit.[26] An exclusive diet of one type of hymn, whatever type that is, will have a cumulative effect on the formation of an individual or congregation, often influencing the way that they most commonly address God in prayer. Childhood memories of how we spoke of

---

24 Unpublished survey of 1347 services in 235 churches, Rosalind Brown, June–November 2000.
25 The four most popular hymns across all churches were *Be still for the presence of the Lord, the Holy One, is here, Praise my soul the king of heaven, Be thou my vision* and *Praise to the Lord, the Almighty, the king of creation.* Among Methodist and United Reformed Churches, *Make me a channel of your peace* was by far the most sung hymn in the survey. The Church of England did not have such a clear front-runner.
26 See Wren, B, *What Language Shall I Borrow* (New York: Crossroad, 1989) for a more detailed analysis of ways of speaking of God in hymns in *Hymns and Psalms—A Methodist and Ecumenical Hymnbook.*

God can be very formative. My earliest memory of a Sunday School song is 'A lamb went a wandering so far from the fold…Good Shepherd is seeking the lamb from the fold,' and the understanding of God as a good shepherd, although added to and enhanced over the years, is still deeply etched in me.

The index can also tell us about the potential formative impact of a hymnal. Hymns that begin not with God but in the first person are more likely (but not inevitably) to place us at the centre of the action. One way of gauging this is to see how many hymns begin the words 'I' or 'we' at the beginning of the text. This is a not fool-proof, but it does highlight trends. Thus the 1982 edition of *Ancient and Modern Revised* contains 636 hymns of which 3% begin in this way. An early evangelical hymn book, *Golden Bells*, includes 738 hymns, of which 7% begin 'I' and a further 3% 'we' (or their derivatives). *Songs of Fellowship*, which is popular across denominations, has 1150 hymns and songs in its 1998 edition, with 11% and 5% beginning 'I/I'm/I've/I'll' and 'we/we're/ we'll/we've.' These last percentages are similar to those in *The Source* (10% and 4%), a 1998 collection of 610 hymns which describes itself as 'the definitive worship collection.' Hymnals from the evangelical / charismatic tradition are more likely to shape devotion in terms of our relationship with God whereas other hymnals more likely to begin with the Christian tradition, only then moving to the human response.

Contrasting Approaches

The two most sung hymns in the recent hymn survey, albeit they were sung less than 1% of the time, were the 1986 text *Be still for the presence of the Lord, the Holy One, is here* and the nineteenth-century text *Praise, my soul, the King of heaven*. One has stood the test of time; the other has yet to prove its staying power. There are many similarities between them that may help to explain both why they are popular and what their formative effects might be.

Both hymns begin by calling on the soul to respond to God, although they then move into a more general first person plural voice that tells of our experience of God at the present moment. God is addressed in each hymn as transcendent (the Holy One, the King of heaven) and spoken of as immanent or intimate (God is here and all around, Father-like). The language of the faith tradition permeates each hymn—the allusion to Moses standing on holy ground and to the Psalmist's 'Be still' in one, our salvation history 'ransomed, healed, restored, forgiven' in the other. This forms the basis of our response to God—we who are in need of cleansing and healing, who are feeble-framed and frail as summer flowers (another biblical allusion to Isaiah 40.6 and Matthew 6.28).

The opening words of each are strong—'Be still!' 'Praise, my soul!' Singers are immediately called to respond, and told how to respond—by bowing before God, by bringing tribute. The hymns begin as worship of God who is greater than we are; our position is submission, and yet neither hymn implies abject fear. One goes on to describe God's holiness and power to a tune that hints at gentleness, the other sings of what God has done for us to a tune that hints at strength. The tune emphasizes the opening words of each and nuances the successive words, while the words are tightly constructed and not wasted.

What are the hymns trying to do? Lest there be any doubt, *Be still* uses the same words at the beginning of each stanza. The words go on to draw us into the biblical story of Moses, which must have been a fearful experience at the time, but then—whilst retaining the awe—moves us to awareness of God's mercy and encourages us to be open to receive from this holy God. There is a sense of delicacy, almost fragility, about this hymn which belies the awe of its theme and makes it unsuitable for boisterous worship or the end of a service. This hymn can work both early in a service, before communion, or in a time of extended singing; in each case it stills its singers, preparing them for encounter with a holy and gracious God. Although it draws on the language of faith, it does so in a way that does not require knowledge of it for the meaning to be clear. It keeps and leaves us in passive, receptive mode before God.

'Praise my soul' is a stronger hymn that keeps returning to the contrast of God's power and our dependence, yet without belittling us or rendering us powerless. Unlike angels we do not yet see God face to face, but we can call on angels and all creation to join the praise of God. The language and experience of faith are presumed and spoken of without elaboration. Despite the references to God's work in and for us, there is no mention of Jesus Christ, or the Holy Spirit, and the overall feel of the hymn is that God is 'other' than us despite all God has done for us. It can be used almost anywhere in a service. Its formative effect, particularly after many singings, is likely to be a reinforcement both of God's otherness and yet God's tenderness for us. It is clearly a corporate hymn, despite beginning in the first person singular.

Why are these hymns popular and how are they formative? They are focused yet range widely; they engage us from the start; they speak the language of faith; they remind us of God's otherness and God's care for us in our need; they develop their theme and move us forward, leading us to respond to God. In neither case do they tie up every last loose end. They leave us standing before the God who has formed and transformed us already—not telling God what to do but open and receptive through our stillness and our adoration.

5
Hymns and Christian Formation

Hymns shape the lives of their singers, both those who sing regularly and also occasional hymn-singers as they sing at particularly significant times in their lives. We need to know what we want hymns to do, and then choose accordingly without losing sight of the overall balance in the service. We are far more likely to find ourselves humming something we sang in church when we go home than we are to find ourselves meditating on a phrase in the sermon. This is not to deny the formative power of sermons but to underscore the often ignored formative power of hymns. Words set to music engage the emotions and lodge in the memory. The refrains of hymns and choruses are even more likely to stick in the mind, simply because they are sung more frequently. This can help where there are people in the congregation who cannot read or for whom English is a second or even foreign language.

Hymns and Private Devotion

Hymns have a continuing place in private devotions, but this is hindered by the current trend in hymn and song books to list hymns alphabetically. For personal devotion, books that adopt a thematic approach are more user-friendly since we can go to the section of the book that relates to our particular focus in prayer. There we may find texts that we have never sung but are nevertheless helpful in prayer, whereas a person with an alphabetical book is limited to words that are already known, unless they have time to read the hymn book cover to cover. A good place to begin to introduce hymns into personal prayer life is with a general hymn book that prints hymns thematically, supplemented by the words of other favourite hymns and choruses. Sharing the hymns that have helped us in our own lives can open up new spiritual resources, particularly for people for whom this is new.

Hymns and Poetry

The poets' task and gift is to use evocative language to give us new perspectives on the familiar and to breathe new life where the familiar has lost its power to grasp our attention. Horace (65–8 BC) considered that poetry should teach and delight. Despite the brilliance of some hymns as theology and poetry, many hymns are of mediocre quality in their content or their poetic structure. Some congregations are treated to language and ideas that enlarge and enrich their understanding of God's beauty and creativity, leading—in the words of Fred Pratt Green's hymn—to 'a more profound alleluia.'[27] Other congregations have

---

27 From the hymn *When in our music God is glorified.*

21

a diet of uninspiring, even tedious and repetitious, verse that does little to convey wonder and anticipation as we come into God's presence. Poor poetry may be the culprit, or the use of platitudes or endless repetition. All this is formative for good or ill.

A good hymn should lift us to God in worship and send us home stimulated to explore ideas that have been sparked or perspectives that have been opened up. Evocative phrases are not the prerogative of older hymns. Graham Kendrick's line, 'hands that flung stars into space,' opens up wonderful images of creation, just as Christina Rossetti did one hundred years earlier for the Incarnation with 'Love came down at Christmas, love incarnate, love divine.'

Broadening Hoizons

Congregations who regularly sing phrases that open up new panoramas and possibilities in their faith, or phrases that strengthen their roots in God, are better equipped to grow and mature than those condemned to sing platitudes or dull phrases which do nothing to uplift or inspire. Is it really good enough that a hymn does no harm? What if congregations only sing hymns that do no harm, but do little good? The cumulative effect of singing needs to be taken into account. The hymn survey shows that some of the most sung hymns convey an impression of the Christian life as a struggle that we participate in with tenacity rather than joy. That may indeed be true at times and these hymns contribute a necessary balance to hymns that are all celebration and peace, but a regular diet of hymns like *Lead us, heavenly Father, lead us* (with its statement that Jesus' life was 'dreary'), *Father, hear the prayer we offer* (which seems oblivious of Psalm 23), *O Jesus, I have promised* and *Thy hand, O God, has guided*—all of which were in the top twenty hymns—can suggest that the Christian life is never other than difficult. A congregation reared on hymns like this may be very faithful, but reticent when called on to celebrate joyfully. Equally, congregations reared on a diet of praise and victory hymns may be slow to bring their own and other people's pain and suffering to worship and action.

Hymns and Choruses

Hymns and choruses differ in their formative potential in one significant way. Choruses, by their brevity, cannot develop ideas but merely state—and perhaps repeat—them, whereas a good hymn will move its singers forward through a train of thought to its resolution. Choruses, even when sung in sequence, tend to repeat the same ideas. That is not to deny the value of choruses, particularly for teaching and reinforcing important aspects of our faith especially to children. But it does mean that they are—on the whole—more monochrome in their content. Careful attention therefore needs to be given to ensure that there is some depth of perspective in the overall selection in any service.

Choruses, because of their brevity, cannot set our discipleship in the broader historical context and tend to focus on the present experience of the singers.

22

This can be seen if *All people that on earth do dwell*, with its five verses that speak of coming into God's presence, tell of God's character and recount God's past acts, is contrasted with *As I come into your presence*, which is on the same theme but only focuses on the present action of the singer. Longer is not necessarily better, particularly if several choruses have been chosen to allow ideas to be developed. However, in this instance although both hymns bring us into God's presence, the length of *All people* also gives the potential to ground the singers and their action in Christian tradition. Hymns probably have more potential than choruses to effect growth in faith, discipleship and amendment of life since they take us through a process of developing understanding to the point of being willing to change in the light of what we have sung.

Formation and Engagement

Why are hymns able to form us in the faith? Hymns insist that we engage with the God to and of whom we sing. When we sing we invest ourselves. The words become not just words, but an expression of the desires of our heart. It is not just our lips but our lives that are engaged if we let the words touch our hearts. Worship is an active and iterative process involving mind, heart and will. As we come before God we are transformed and reformed by the Holy Spirit.

Hymns are both text and music, although the focus here has been on text. Too many strong texts are matched with weak tunes, while weak texts remain in use because the tune is beloved of congregations. A change of tune can enable familiar words to touch us and challenge us in new ways. The effect of a hymn is more than the sum of its component parts of text and tune: they have a multiplying effect on each other. Timothy Hone has written that music 'can cause the text to be heard afresh, evoking new associations and enabling new meanings to be found...At its most profound, music is capable of giving new meaning to the incarnate word.'[28]

Facts and Feelings

Words tend to engage the left side of our brain, particularly where they explore theological ideas and ask for our reasoned commitment, whereas music more readily engages the right side of the brain, the world of emotions and intuitive response.[29] A good hymn or chorus therefore brings together both left and right brain, allowing for their integration in worship. Private prayer can draw more from the more feeling-based texts (for example, *Jesus, the very thought of thee*) without losing an overall integration. However, feeling-based texts when

28 Hone, T, 'When in our Music God is Glorified' in Astley, J, Hone, T and Savage, S (eds) *Creative Chords: Studies in Music, Theology and Christian Formation* (Leominster: Gracewing, 2000) p 157.
29 The impact of music on the right side of the brain is referred to in the chapter by J Astley and M Savage, 'Music and Christian Learning' in Astley, J, Hone, T, and Savage, M, *Creative Chords, op cit*, pp 222–224.

sung to tunes that engender emotion (and not all do to the same extent), particularly in a large gathering which adds its own emotional dimension, move us much further into the right-brain world of emotions and away from the integration of head and heart. That is not a reason for avoiding singing these texts, but an observation about their potential effect which can be seen in much charismatic and revivalist worship. Equally, this explains why some hymns seem so 'dry'—they are heavily left-brain texts sung to uninspiring tunes that leave our emotions cold. Too many of those, and our hearts will shrivel. What is needed, for formation purposes, is an integration of mind and heart, will and emotion.

Hymns are essentially a particular genre of poetry, linked with music. On both counts they are a form of art. In an interview primarily about visual art, Frank Burch Brown said words that are also true of poetry and music, 'It is a testimony to the power of art that it can move people in a particularly direct way, more than traditionally it has any right to.'[30] Add in the fact that hymns unite us with the living God, and it is no wonder that hymns not only express human praise and prayer to God, but have a formative power in the lives of the people who sing them. We ignore this at our peril and enter into it for our good. We need to be attentive to what we embed in our memory—we may find ourselves living it one day!

30 *Art and Christian Enquiry Bulletin*, No 25, January 2001.

24